Discover Sheffield

Sheena Woodhead & Melvyn Jones

▲ **Hallam University** In the shape of four drums and made from stainless steel, Sheffield Hallam University students' union complex was originally the National Centre for Popular Music.

▼ **Sheaf Square** The dramatic water features on Sheaf Square in front of the city railway station provide a magnificent gateway to Sheffield for those arriving by train.

CONTENTS

MYRIAD

LONDON

The Heart of the City

Sheffield's city centre is dotted with landmarks old and new such as Kemsley House, the Cathedral, the Town Hall, the Lyceum and Crucible theatres and the City Hall. The £130m "Heart of the City" scheme has transformed part of the southern section of the city centre, with the opening of the Millennium Galleries, the Winter Garden, the re-designed Peace Gardens and a new hotel and office block. Soon The Moor, a southern extension of the central retail area, is to be changed out of all recognition by the building of the Sevenstone retail centre between Moorhead, Pinstone Street and Barker's Pool and the relocation of the market quarter from Castlegate to The Moor.

▶ **The Cathedral** The Church of St Peter and St Paul, Sheffield's medieval parish church, became Sheffield cathedral in 1914. The present church initially dates from the early 15th century, replacing an earlier church probably of early 12th century origin. The crossing tower surmounted by its crocketed spire is an important local landmark. The church was restored between 1878-80 by local architects Flockton & Gibbs with advice from Sir George Gilbert Scott. Ambitious 20th-century plans in the inter-war and post-war period to make the church more "cathedral-like" were only partially completed. The most interesting part of the interior is the Shrewsbury Chapel that contains the tombs of the 4th Earl of Shrewsbury (died 1538) lying between his two wives and the 6th Earl of Shrewsbury. In the churchyard is a monument to James Montgomery (1771-1854), newspaper editor and proprietor, campaigner, poet and hymn-writer. He campaigned for many years against slavery and the employment of young children as chimney sweeps and wrote the hymn *Angels from the Realms of Glory*.

◀ **Kemsley House** Among the best-known Sheffield landmarks on High Street (in a reflection, left) is the former *Sheffield Daily Telegraph* building. It was completed in 1916 and is faced with white faience. The portico is surmounted by a statue of Mercury, the Roman god of eloquence, commerce and messenger of the gods.

◀ **Town Hall** Opened in 1897, the Town Hall was described by Sir Nikolaus Pevsner as "a large picturesque pile". (For more on the Town Hall, see page 7.)

▶ **Paradise Square** Behind the Cathedral lies Paradise Square, a throwback to Georgian Sheffield. Built on a sloping cornfield called Hick's Stile Field it dates from 1736-1790. Among its residents in the early 19th century was Sir Francis Chantrey (1781-1841), who as a child was a milkboy bringing milk, butter and eggs for sale from his father's farm in Derbyshire. He became the chosen sculptor of the great and the good of every walk of life. Paradise Square was a popular venue for gatherings and on 15 July, 1779, John Wesley, the founder of Methodism, preached to a large crowd in the square, recording in his diary that it was "the largest congregation I ever saw on a week-day".

▶ **Fargate** Lying at the heart of Sheffield's retail quarter and now pedestrianised, Fargate has an ancient name. "Gate" is from the Old Norse *gata* meaning a street or a lane, so the full name means the furthest extension southwards of the town from the direction of the castle at the junction of the rivers Don and Sheaf, where the town originated in the 12th century.

▶ **The Yorkshire Bank** This five-storey building occupies the corner of Fargate and Surrey Street. It has some carved winged lions and human figures around its balustraded balcony and there are carved gargoyles. The building used to have a temperance restaurant and hotel (the Albany Hotel) on its upper floors. The second particularly interesting building is numbers 38-40 (now WH Smith's) built in the Gothic style in the early 1880s. It was built for Arthur Davy, provisioner, and carries, appropriately enough, above the third floor the carved heads of a sheep, pig, cow and ox, the main constituents of his meat counters.

▲ **Orchard Square** This extension to the central shopping area at the top of Fargate opened in 1987. It is in the form of a courtyard with access to Church Street beyond to the north and Leopold Street to the west. The clocktower in Orchard Square pays homage to Sheffield's industrial past with its working figures of a grinder and a buffer girl.

◀ **Leopold Street** This late Victorian street was named after Prince Leopold, Queen Victoria's youngest son who in 1879 paid an official visit to open Firth College, forerunner of the University of Sheffield, the new building being the square stone building at the far end of the street (right-hand side of the photograph left). Attached to Firth College is what in Edwardian times were the former School Board offices and the Boys' Central Schools. The Central Higher School (opened in 1880) was the first of its kind in the country. The whole block was for many years the City of Sheffield's education offices. Now the building has been transformed into a 90-bedroom luxury hotel, the Leopold, together with a number of restaurants and bars, that opened in 2007.

◀ ▲ **Church Street** To the west of the Cathedral precinct in Church Street stands the Gladstone Buildings built in 1885 as the Reform Club. The second and third floor rooms were the main club rooms and included a dining room, library and lounge. Gothic in style, it is built of red brick with stone dressings, tall mullioned windows, turrets and dormers. Across Church Street stands the Cutlers' Hall, headquarters of the Company of Cutlers in Hallamshire (left) which came into being in 1624. The present hall, in Grecian style with four Corinthian columns, was the third hall to be built for the Cutlers and was completed in 1832 and extended in 1888. Church Street is a busy route for the Supertram system. This was completed between 1994 and 1995 with routes extending to Middlewood and Malin Bridge in the north, Halfway, Herdings and Crystal Peaks in the south-east and Meadowhall Shopping Centre in the east.

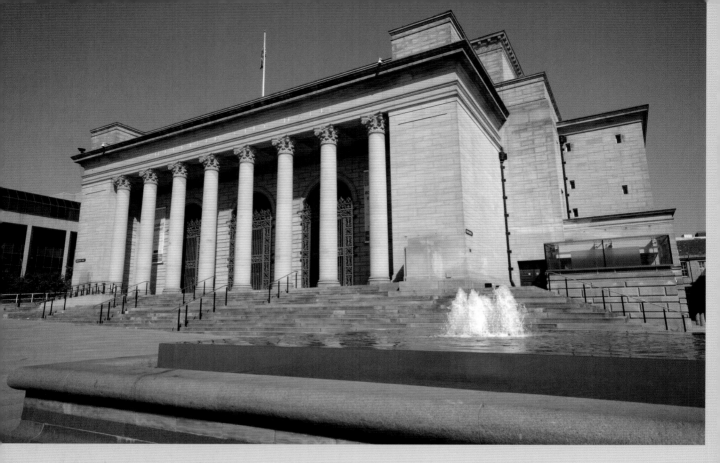

The City Hall Opened in 1932, the City Hall was originally designed as early as 1920, by E Vincent Harris, but construction did not begin until 1929. It has been completely refurbished at a cost of over £12m. Constructed from stone quarried in Darley Dale, Derbyshire, it is in the Classical Revival style dominated by a portico with eight Corinthian columns. Originally conceived as a memorial hall to the city's First World War dead it became Sheffield's main concert hall with a memorial hall (right) at the rear. The main hall accommodates 2,800 people.

Barker's Pool This open space in front of the City Hall has a most interesting history. Lying beyond the end of Fargate in the medieval period was an area known as Balm Green which contained Barker's Pool, which really was a pool, a source of fresh water to supplement the supply from public and private wells until 1793. Details of minor improvements made to Barker's Pool survive from as early as 1572 when it was walled, "feyed" (ie cleaned) and a new bolt was fixed to the shuttle. The shuttle (a sluice gate) would have been an important feature when water from the pool was occasionally released and channelled through the town to clean its streets, eventually finding its way down into the river Don. The pool also contained at one period the town's "cucking stool", for ducking women and other objectionable persons who spread malicious gossip!

Ceremonial Since 1925 Barker's Pool has been the venue for a memorial service on Remembrance Day, and in 1945 it was the scene of jubilant celebrations to mark the end of the war in Europe (VE Day). Now every year in late November it is full of students and their families during Sheffield Hallam University's degree conferment ceremony in the City Hall. When the City Hall was recently refurbished Barker's Pool was re-paved and two new fountains were installed.

War Memorial This memorial, to the 5,000 men who died in the First World War, was unveiled in 1925 and arose from a competition announced a year earlier. The competition was won by CD Carus Wilson, head of the University of Sheffield's School of Architecture. It is in the form of a steel pole rising 90ft (27m) from a bronze base. The pole is surrounded by the life-size figures of four soldiers sculpted by George Alexander.

Town Hall The centre of Sheffield is dominated by the Town Hall, built of Derbyshire sandstone, standing at the junction of Surrey Street and Pinstone Street. Designed by EW Mountford, it was opened by Queen Victoria in 1897. After opening the Town Hall she was driven to Norfolk Park where 50,000 children had been assembled to sing to the queen. The visit ended with a trip to Charles Cammell's Cyclops steelworks. Reflecting Sheffield's industrial history there are two friezes carved in stone around the exterior walls of the Town Hall which depict, among other things, grinders, smiths, smelters and miners. The 200ft tower is surmounted by an 8ft high bronze statue of Vulcan, the Roman god of fire and furnaces, with his right foot on an anvil and pincers in his left hand. Inside is a life-size statue of the Duke of Norfolk and a bust of Queen Victoria.

Peace Gardens These gardens in Sheffield's most central civic space occupy the site of St Paul's Church. This church was begun in 1720 but did not open until 1740. This was because of an argument between the donor of £10,000 for its construction, John Downes, a goldsmith, and the church authorities, about the right of appointment of a curate. The church was demolished in 1937. The site was cleared in the same year to make a public open space named to commemorate the peace expected from the Munich agreement of 1938. The gardens were redesigned in 1997-98 as part of the "Heart of the City" project. An interesting feature of the newly-designed space are bronze vessels from which water overflows and runs down tiled cascades. They are said to represent the rivers on which Sheffield's early prosperity was based.

▲ ▶ The Winter Garden This is the green heart of Sheffield, the crowning glory of the £120m "Heart of the City" project. It is a place for office workers and shoppers to meet or relax and combines stunning architecture with a unique collection of plants. The new structure was opened in December 2002 with a children's candlelight procession and fireworks and within a year it had attracted more than 1m visitors. It is 230ft (70m) long and 72ft (22m) wide and its arched structure is formed by 10 pairs of parabolic wooden arches that reach up to 72ft (22m). Made of larch, the arches require no preservative coatings and will mature to a silvery grey colour. The Winter Garden is a temperate glasshouse with the temperature kept constant, frost kept at bay and humidity closely controlled. This is achieved in a number of ways. The building is glazed with more than 1,400 glass panels of which 128 open and close automatically. Fans move concentrations of hot air in summer which is then released through the vents. Underfloor heating protects the plants from frost and small water features control levels of humidity. The Winter Garden houses 2,500 plants of over 150 species mainly from the Southern Hemisphere including palms from Madagascar, grasses and trees from Australia and pines from Norfolk Island. Most of the plants bloom in winter – hence the name Winter Garden!

Tudor Square Lying at the centre of Sheffield's cultural life, Tudor Square is bounded on the north by the Crucible Theatre, on the south by the entrance to the Winter Garden, on the east by the Lyceum Theatre (below) and the Central Library and Graves Art Gallery (left) and on the west by bars and restaurants. The Crucible Theatre, built in 1969-70, is not very eye-catching from the outside, but inside things are very different. The auditorium has a central thrust stage almost surrounded by banks of seating for an audience of 1,000. Under the same roof, the Crucible Studio Theatre holds an audience of 400 people completely in the round. The Central Library and Graves Art Gallery, in Portland stone, were built between 1929 and 1934. The Graves Art Gallery was the gift of Alderman JG Graves who also donated 400 paintings and drawings.

The Lyceum Theatre Built in 1893 as the City Theatre, it was partially destroyed in a fire in 1896, and under new ownership was re-modelled in 1897 by the theatre architect WGR Sprague. The Lyceum is thought to be the only surviving example of Sprague's work outside London. The exterior of the theatre has stucco decoration and a corner dome surmounted by a figure of Mercury. But it was the interior of the theatre, the auditorium, that was magnificent. The walls were covered in fine plasterwork, cherubs separated painted panels, the proscenium arch was surrounded by rococo plasterwork, above was a beautiful ceiling and all was lit by the most advanced form of gas lighting. The theatre was sympathetically restored, inside and out in 1989-90. It is now the venue for West End touring productions, operas by Opera North and local productions.

Millennium Galleries Completed in 2001 as part of the "Heart of the City" project, the Millennium Galleries have three complementary roles. First and foremost they extend the city's museum space by nearly 2,000 square metres; together with the adjoining Winter Garden, they form an interesting covered section on the route from the railway station and Sheffield Hallam University to the urban centre; and the Azure café is a pleasant space in which to have a refreshing drink or snack. The Millennium Galleries face onto Arundel Gate with the café on the ground floor. The galleries occupy the upper floor and are reached from Arundel Gate by escalator. Along with temporary exhibitions there is a permanent space for Sheffield's metalwork and silverware collection and the Ruskin Collection. This the property of the Guild of St George, an organisation set up by John Ruskin to broaden the minds of working people, that established its first museum in Sheffield in 1875.

Fitzalan Square So-called after one of the family names of the Dukes of Norfolk, the major private landowner in Sheffield, Fitzalan Square was laid out over a protracted period from 1869 to 1881. Early 20th century photographs of the square show it as an important tram terminus crowded with waiting horse cabs. At its centre is a bronze statue of King Edward VII dating from 1913 by Alfred Drury. On the pedestal are scenes representing Philanthropy, Peace and Unity. The Philanthropy scene shows human figures holding aloft a model of the King Edward VII Hospital.

▲ **Victoria Hall** A striking building on Norfolk Street is the Methodist Victoria Hall. Built in brick and stone in a mixture of Gothic and Arts & Crafts styles it was completed in 1908. It has a tall square tower with a large Baroque top and interesting carved decoration, including carvings of John and Charles Wesley. The hall has recently undergone a thorough refurbishment. The first phase completed in 2005 included a new reception area, lifts and easier access for visitors with mobility problems. The second phase included cleaning the facade, creating a new lounge at the rear of the worship room and opening a new café.

Castle House This large store, standing at the junction of Angel Street and Castle Street, was built between 1959 and 1964 for Brightside and Carbrook Co-operative Society. It was also the society's headquarters. It replaced an early large store on Exchange Street that was very badly damaged during the Blitz of 1940. Castle House was the Sheffield Co-operative Society's department store until the spring of 2008. An unusual feature of the store is the spiral staircase, cantilevered, with banisters of stainless steel leading to a glass dome. On the wall facing King Street is a figure representing Vulcan, the Roman god of fire, whose most ancient festival was the Fornacalia, held in his honour as god of furnaces. He holds a special place in the history of Sheffield, once known as "Steel City" and also appears on top of the Town Hall as an 8ft high bronze statue.

Sheffield Hallam University This is one of the "new" universities created in 1992 from Sheffield City Polytechnic. Until the 1970s there were a number of colleges in the Sheffield region, each with their own culture and ethos. On the Pond Street site, now the City Campus, was the College of Technology that was created in 1950 and which occupied an expanding site built between 1953 and 1968. In 1969 the College of Technology merged with the College of Art which occupied a site on Psalter Lane two miles to the south-west of the city centre, to form Sheffield Polytechnic. The varied origins and specialisms of its component parts has meant that Sheffield Hallam University, from its outset, has been able to offer a wide range of undergraduate and postgraduate degree courses. It prides itself on its close links with employers, and a greater percentage of students than at any other British university are on courses with a work placement.

Around the Heart of the City

In the 19th and the first half of the 20th century the areas around Sheffield city centre consisted of streets of back-to-back and terraced housing. Most of this has now been demolished and replaced by tower blocks and other high-rise developments. In recent years city centre living has become popular and new apartment blocks have been built on old industrial sites, especially along waterfronts, and disused factories and warehouses converted to residential use. Major sporting venues such as Ponds Forge International Leisure Centre and Bramall Lane football ground also lie close to the city centre.

▶ **Park Hill Flats** High above the Sheaf valley stand the Park Hill flats, Sheffield's "streets in the sky". These flats, acclaimed by architects and sociologists in their early days, have also been referred to by other experts as extreme examples of Sixties' architectural brutalism. They are now Grade II (starred) listed and a refurbishment scheme has been agreed to transform the complex into upmarket apartments, rented flats and small business premises. Below are the Hyde Park flats that stand to the north of the Park Hill flats overlooking the confluence of the Don and Sheaf. They are the re-clad two remaining tower blocks of the original three. Completed in 1966, the central block was demolished in 1992 and the two remaining blocks were taken back to their concrete frameworks and re-clad in red and yellow brick. Behind the re-clad blocks can just be seen the spire of St John's church (1836-38) which originally stood among tightly-packed back-to-back houses.

◀ ▼ **Railway Station** Sheffield did not get a direct railway route to London until 1870 when the first station on this site was built. Before then a railway journey to London involved a trip to Rotherham on the Sheffield and Rotherham Railway, then a train on the Midland Railway's line from York to London via Derby. This was to avoid the broad ridge between Sheffield and Chesterfield to the south that would have required very deep cuttings. Instead George Stephenson took the line to Rotherham through the Rother valley where the gradients were easier. The 1870 line to Chesterfield breaches the high ridge via the Bradway tunnel. The present station, still known to many as the "Midland Station", is the creation of Charles Trubshaw in 1905; some of the 1870 station still survives on platform 2.

Sheaf Square Visitors arriving in Sheffield by train in the last few years have seen tremendous changes. Not only has the station itself been refurbished but the townscape outside has been transformed. Gone is the roundabout at the bottom of Howard Street, the office blocks of Sheaf House and Dyson House have been demolished, the line of Sheaf Street has been re-aligned and immediately in front of the station a new public square, Sheaf Square, has been created. This has water features, trees and public seating. On the edge of the square beside Sheaf Street is a stainless steel sculpture – the Cutting Edge. The sculpture and the station façade are all illuminated at night. Stainless steel was a Sheffield invention in 1913. The discoverer of stainless steel, a chromium steel that almost completely resists corrosion, was Harry Brearley. Locally-born (in Ramsden's Yard, off the Wicker) he rose from being a bottle-washer to director of Brown-Firth's research laboratories.

▲ **SHU Students' Union Building** This building is peculiarly shaped because it was the short-term home of the National Centre for Popular Music. It is in the shape of four drums of stainless steel, each drum tilted outwards. Funded by a large Lottery grant, it was completed in 1998. The Centre for Popular Music had a short life and after lying vacant for a time it was acquired in 2003 by Sheffield Hallam University for use as the students' union building. It now contains a ground-floor public bar serving hot foods and snacks throughout the day, a shop and a student bar, as well as meeting rooms for clubs and societies. The exterior is polished about once a year.

◀ **The Persistence Works** Located on Brown Street, the Persistence Works is a new building that contains studios for craftspeople and artists, members of the Yorkshire Artspace Society (YAS). Constructed from concrete it consists of a low block with a six-storey block behind and was completed in 2001; it incorporated seven artists' commissions in its design. Brown Street is located in an area to the south-east of the city centre that has now been designated as the Cultural Industries Quarter. Originally laid out in the late 18th century and subsequently occupied by cutlers' workshops and metalworking businesses the area has now been colonised by small and medium-sized enterprises in the arts, communications and media.

▶ Bramall Lane Lying immediately to the south of the city centre, Bramall Lane is the home of Sheffield United, the "Blades". Yorkshire County Cricket Club was founded in Sheffield in 1863 and County matches were played at Bramall Lane for more than a century. It became Sheffield United's football ground in 1889. The Blades were the Football League Division 1 Champions in 1897-98 only seven years after being elected to Division 2. Their early record in the FA Cup is outstanding: they were winners in 1899, 1902, 1915 and 1925 and runners-up in 1901 and 1936.

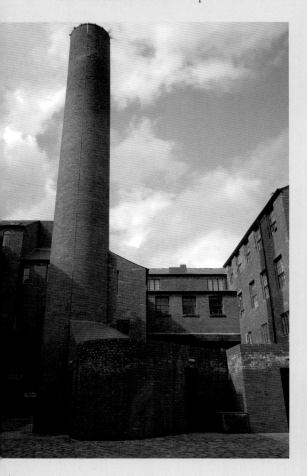

▶ Devonshire Green The now fashionable Devonshire Quarter between the city centre and the University of Sheffield is a part of the inner city that has seen the development of some large-scale residential building in recent years. The green itself was a bombed part of the city during the Second World War that was never built on again and which has now been transformed into a modern public open space with colourful planting. To the west of the green (in the background) is the prestigious West One development consisting of 500 apartments with restaurants, cafés and bars.

▼ The Somme Barracks Dating from 1907 the Somme Barracks were built for the West Yorkshire Royal Engineers Volunteers. The gatehouse has a high and wide arched doorway below a tower with a mullioned and transom window and above that the name, then the royal coat of arms before reaching the top surmounted by two small turrets. Further along West Street are the Cavendish Buildings which also date from 1907. They were built as a garage and showroom for the Sheffield Motor Company. The faience-covered three-storey façade has mullioned windows and the roofline is broken by four elaborate pediments with the building's dates.

▲ Butcher's Wheel In 1893, White's Sheffield Directory listed 281 table knife manufacturers, 125 scissors-makers, and 128 electro-plate and nickel-silver makers. Butcher's Wheel on Arundel Street is one of the best of the few still surviving Victorian cutlery, edge tool and file-making works in Sheffield. This brick-built works extending to four storeys was constructed in the mid-19th century by William and Samuel Butcher. Unused for a long time and recently refurbished it still manages to exude a sense of Dickensian working conditions. The large first and second floor casements were designed to shed maximum light on the "grinding hulls" that occupied those floors.

▶ ▼ The University of Sheffield Officially opened by King Edward VII on 12 July 1905, the new university had started life as a university college in 1897, being an amalgamation of Firth College (which became the School of Arts & Science), the Medical Institution (which became the Medical School) and the Technical School (which became the School of Technology). The commitment to gain full university status had been spurred on when it was mooted that the University College of Leeds should become the University of Yorkshire. The new red brick university buildings, Firth Court (below), at Western Bank beside Weston Park, were designed by Mitchell Gibbs in the Tudor style. Dominating the Western Bank campus today is the 21-storey Arts Tower, which was completed in 1965. Considerable refurbishment is now planned. The building currently contains two conventional lifts and a "paternoster" lift. The latter, open-doored and in continual motion up and down, is said to have deterred some prospective students from taking up the place offered to them! The University of Sheffield, which has 26,000 students, has an enviable reputation. In 2001 it won *The Sunday Times* University of the Year award and was described by *The Times* as one of the powerhouses of British higher education.

▶ **Cornish Place Works**
Viewed from Ball Street Bridge, this was the factory of James Dixon & Sons, manufacturer of silverware, silver plate and Britannia metal goods. Founded in 1805, the firm moved to Cornish Place in 1822. At the beginning of the 20th century James Dixon had a workforce of more than 900 but by the 1990s the firm had ceased to exist and the works were converted into apartments in 1998. Ball Street Bridge (right) was re-built after the Great Sheffield Flood of 11 March 1864 that caused the death of 240 people. The bridge collapsed from the weight of the machinery and timber brought down by flood water that battered its arches.

◀ **Cementation Furnace** Until the second half of the 18th century the steel used by Sheffield's cutlers was either imported or was locally made "shear steel" which was forged from "blister steel" made in a cementation furnace. Some 260 such furnaces, easily recognised by their conical chimneys, were eventually built in Sheffield, of which only one survives, on Hoyle Street (left). Alternate layers of charcoal and iron bars covered by a layer of mortar were placed in two sandstone chests inside a cementation furnace. The furnace was sealed and a coal fire lit below the chests which burned for seven to nine days. The iron bars now converted to blister steel (they were covered in small blisters) were then made into shear steel by being heated in bundles to bright red and then forged into a uniform bar.

▶ **Kelham Island Industrial Museum** Opened in 1982, the museum, which tells the story of Sheffield's industrial development, occupies the old electricity generating station for the electric tramway system. The visitor is greeted by the sight of a Bessemer converter. The Bessemer converter made its first appearance on Carlisle Street at Bessemer's Steel Works in 1858. This was a radical step by its inventor Henry Bessemer since the new invention was greeted with scepticism by the rather conservative Sheffield steel producers who were doubtful about the quality of the large amounts of steel that were produced in a short space of time. Bessemer, the outsider, saw his new works initially as a place of demonstration for potential licensees. Two of Sheffield's major firms, John Brown's and Charles Cammell's, became the earliest converts and produced their first Bessemer steel rails in 1861, followed by Samuel Fox in 1863.

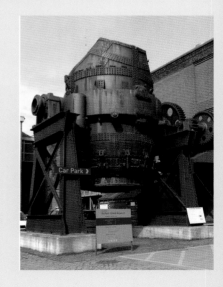

▲ **Aizlewood's Mill** The Don valley to the north-west of the city centre has a mixture of newbuilds and refurbished industrial buildings. Aizlewood's Mill (the Crown Flour Mills) is located on Nursery Street north of the river Don. Standing six storeys high with a tall rectangular-shaped chimney, the mill has now been converted into offices and workshops.

◀▶ **Victoria Quays** In the 17th and 18th centuries, Sheffield's steel products were transported by packhorse to the ports of Yorkshire and Lancashire. Goods for the London and European market went to the river port of Bawtry where they were transferred to barges and carried down the river Idle to the Trent and the port of Hull. The inconvenience and slowness of the overland journey from Sheffield to Bawtry led the Cutlers Company to explore the possibility of making the Don navigable from Doncaster to Sheffield and in 1726 an Act of Parliament was passed and work began. But it proved impracticable to extend the waterway and so Tinsley remained the terminus from 1751 until 1819 when the Sheffield canal opened, terminating at the Canal Basin near the junction of the Sheaf and Don. The extension of the canal into Sheffield was greeted with acclaim and a fleet of barges with flags and bands made a triumphal entry into the Canal Basin. The Basin was refurbished, renamed the Victoria Quays and opened by the Prince of Wales in 1994. Shown here are the restored Coal Merchants' Offices (left) and the Straddle Warehouse (right).

The Suburbs

The pre-twentieth century residential and industrial suburbs of Sheffield were largely in the outlying townships of the former medieval parish – to the west in Nether Hallam and Upper Hallam, to the south and south-west in Ecclesall and in the east and north-east in Attercliffe cum Darnall and Brightside. Norton was annexed from Derbyshire in 1901, Stannington was incorporated gradually between 1901 and 1914, Handsworth in 1920, and Dore and Totley, like Norton formerly part of Derbyshire, between 1929 and 1934. In 1967 another part of Derbyshire, Mosborough, became part of the city and after the reorganisation of local government in 1974 the former West Riding County Council communities of Bradfield, Stocksbridge, Oughtibridge, Worrall, Grenoside, High Green, Chapeltown and Ecclesfield became part of Sheffield.

Below, the Gleadless Valley, built in the 1950s and 1960s, one of the biggest public housing developments in the country.

▲ King Edward VII School

Designed by William Flockton (born 1804) and built between 1837-40 as the Wesley Proprietary Grammar School, later the Wesley College, this handsome school is known to locals as "King Ted's". With his partners and his son, Thomas, Flockton designed a number of fine buildings in Sheffield. These include the New Chapel in the General Cemetery, Kenwood, the home of George Wostenholm, cutlery manufacturer and the houses of three of Sheffield's most successful steel magnates: Tapton Hall, for Edward Vickers, Oakbrook for Sir John Brown and Endcliffe Hall for Mark Firth.

▲◀ Norton Church

Norton was part of Derbyshire until 1901 and the centre still has a village atmosphere with its obelisk to the sculptor, Sir Francis Chantrey, who was born in the parish, its war memorial, the rectory and the medieval church. The church, St James', is a combination of styles: the exterior is mainly Perpendicular but it includes a restored Norman south doorway and a mainly Early English tower. Inside the church there is a fine early 16th century alabaster monument of William Blythe and his wife. It is said that it was the Blythe tomb in Norton church that kindled Chantrey's interest in sculpture.

▼ Sharrow Snuff Mill

The water-powered site on the river Porter occupied by Wilson's Sharrow Snuff Mill has been in operation since at least the late 16th century. A new snuff mill was built in 1763 and has been run by the Wilson family ever since. By the early 19th century the waterwheel was joined by a steam engine in the production process. Although no longer used in snuff production, the whole water-power system is still in place: a weir on the river Porter deflects the water to the building.

Beauchief Abbey Formerly in that part of north Derbyshire that became part of Sheffield in 1901, the name "Beauchief" is Norman-French and means "beautiful headland". It is pronounced "Bee-chif". The abbey was founded between 1173 and 1176 by Robert Fitzranulf, lord of the manor of Norton and Alfreton, for the Premonstratensians who were known as the White Canons and were noted for founding their monastic houses in isolated locations and living in poverty.

Abbeydale Industrial Hamlet This is the best preserved water-powered industrial site in Sheffield and is managed by the Sheffield Industrial Museums Trust. The works were the site of a scythemaking business from 1714 until 1935 and before that there is circumstantial evidence that it was a lead-smelting mill. The method of harnessing water power, clearly exemplified at Abbeydale, was that a weir was built to deflect water from the river, in this case the river Sheaf, into a reservoir, locally called a dam, via a channel called a goit or leat. By the end of the 18th century there were 130 water-powered sites on Sheffield's rivers.

Dore & Totley Travel just a short distance up the A621 (Baslow Road) beyond the post office in Totley and you are in the Peak District National Park. Now a busy suburb in south Sheffield, Totley, like its neighbour Dore (left), was until the late 1920s part of north Derbyshire. The most historic part of the village is still characterised by cottages and farmsteads built of the warm local gritstone. Perhaps the oldest building in the village is Totley Old Hall, parts of which date from 1623 (there is a datestone above the doorway) but there were substantial alterations and additions in the Victorian period. The last private owner was William Aldam Milner who lived there from the 1880s until his death in 1931. The Hall has since been converted into apartments.

▼ Ringinglow Roundhouse This tollhouse, the best-known surviving tollhouse in Sheffield, was located at a junction on the turnpike road system where the roughly east-west Sheffield-Hathersage-Chapel-en-le-Frith road met the road turning south to the Fox Inn and on towards Buxton. By the 18th century road traffic was increasing so much that the ancient system of parishes or townships being responsible for the maintenance of highways within their jurisdiction could not cope. The system of turnpikes therefore came into being on which tolls were charged at tollgates. The roundhouse at Ringinglow is actually octagonal in shape and allowed the toll-keeper to have clear views of traffic approaching the gates in all directions. The roundhouse operated as a toll-keeper's house from 1795 to 1825.

▲ Fulwood Old Chapel This Unitarian place of worship is simple but appealing and dates from 1728. Money to build "a large and handsome Chapel" was left in the will of Fulwood resident William Ronksley. It has an adjoining schoolroom and at the rear is the old Chapel House where the minister once resided. In the chapel garden are the old village stocks.

▶ Ecclesfield Church

St Mary's church, Ecclesfield was largely rebuilt between 1480 and 1520. It stands on the site of a much earlier Christian shrine that gave the original village its name. The name Ecclesfield means an open space in an otherwise well-wooded area ("field"), in which stood a Christian church (*ecclesia*). In the churchyard is buried Alexander John Scott (1768-1840), Nelson's chaplain at Trafalgar.

▼ Hillsborough Barracks

Located between Langsett Road and Penistone Road in Hillsborough, Hillsborough Barracks were built in the early 1850s following the Chartist demonstrations of the 1840s. Originally the barracks included quarters for officers and their servants, a chapel, a hospital, infantry soldiers' quarters, cavalry soldiers' quarters and a school for 80 children.

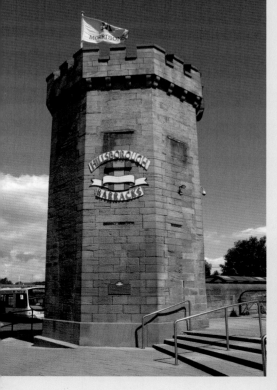

▼ Hillsborough Football Ground

The home ground of Sheffield Wednesday FC, nicknamed "The Owls". The club was founded in 1867 as the football side of Wednesday Cricket Club. After playing in different locations, Hillsborough became the club's ground in 1899, but did not take its modern name of Hillsborough until 1914. The record attendance at the ground was nearly 73,000 in 1934. The capacity of today's all-seater stadium is nearly 40,000. Wednesday have a fine League and Cup record, being Division 1 champions in 1902-03, 1903-04, 1928-29 and 1929-30 and FA Cup winners in 1896, 1907 and 1935.

▶ Hallam FC

Sandygate's main claim to fame is that it is the home of Hallam FC. Founded on 4 September 1860, Hallam FC is recognised as being one of the oldest football clubs in the world. This honour does not quite match the fame of its close rival Sheffield FC which is the oldest football club in the world, having been founded in 1857. Hallam FC still play at the same ground, on Sandygate Road, Crosspool, which according to the *Guinness Book of Records* is the oldest football ground in the world.

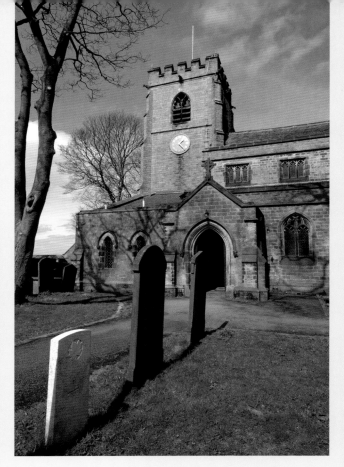

Bolsterstone This small Pennine village lies at nearly 1000ft (306m) between the industrial town of Stocksbridge to the north and Broomhead and More Hall reservoirs in the Ewden valley to the south. The village is home to the famous Bolsterstone Male Voice Choir. Founded in 1934, the nucleus of the new choir came from the church choir.

▼ **Stocksbridge Clock Tower** Stocksbridge was a Victorian industrial community created around Samuel Fox's steelworks. Fox amassed fortunes from umbrella frames and steel rails. Built between 1920 and 1923 as a war memorial, the Clock Tower's construction was funded by public subscription and built on land granted by RHR Rimington Wilson of nearby Broomhead Hall.

▲ **St James' Chapel, Midhopestones** Perched above the Little Don valley to the west of Stocksbridge (formerly on the northern edge of the extensive ancient parish of Ecclesfield), is St James' Chapel in the village of Midhopestones. The "hop" in Midhopestones means a small enclosed valley as in Glossop and Worksop. The medieval chapel-of-ease that existed here was re-built in 1705 by Godfrey Bosville, as the initials and date on the wall show. Bosville was the lord of the manor and resided at Gunthwaite Hall six miles (10 km) to the north where he also had a deer park. The chapel is a tiny building constructed of local gritstone with a stone slate roof. It has plain mullioned windows and a small bell turret with a pyramidal top. Inside there is a Jacobean pulpit. The chapel still contains the original pews and the west gallery built by Bosville.

▲▲ **Meadowhall** Dominating the eastern end of the Lower
Don valley, beside the M1 motorway and on the site formerly
occupied by Hadfield's East Hecla steelworks, is the American-
style enclosed Meadowhall Shopping Centre, with its 1.2m sq ft
of shopping space, 270 stores and free parking for 12,000 cars.
At very busy times the shopping centre is called by locals
"Medderhell". The phenomenal success of Meadowhall has
enticed further development along the Don valley corridor.
The landmark Tinsley Towers (the cooling towers of the former
Blackburn Meadows Power Station) were demolished on 24
August 2008, 30 years after they had stopped working. They
had been part of the Sheffield landscape since 1938 and for
Sheffielders returning to the city via the M1 motorway they were
a welcome sign of home. They stood just 39ft (12m) from the
M1. They are now sorely missed by many people.

◄ Lower Don Valley Industry For 120 years the Lower Don valley was the city's industrial heartland. This powerhouse of industry was laid waste by the recession of the early 1980s. Sheffield Forgemasters (left), created from the merging of some of the most famous names in the industry, managed to keep its head above water and now is a prosperous concern.

▼ River Don Works The offices of Vickers' River Don works, dating from 1906, once the hub of a mighty business concern, now lie empty and for sale. The firm was founded by Sheffield-born Edward Vickers who took over the steel firm of Naylor, Vickers & Co at Millsands in 1867 and moved to the River Don Works in Brightside. The firm manufactured steel, armaments, ships and aircraft parts.

◄ Leisure and sports facilities
Three sporting arenas have made important contributions to the regeneration of the Lower Don valley: the Don Valley Stadium, the largest athletics stadium in the UK; the English Institute of Sport which provides state-of-the-art facilities and support services for world-class athletes, and iceSheffield (left) which contains two Olympic-size ice rinks and seating for 1,500 spectators. The nearby Arena holds 12,000 people and hosts concerts by international pop stars. It is the home of Sheffield Steelers ice hockey team. Described by various architectural writers as "hulking", "dreary" and "dull" it was opened in 1991 for the World Student Games. The bridge over Coleridge Road that links the Arena with iceSheffield and the Don Valley Stadium is an attractive addition to the Lower Don valley landscape.

Sheffield's Urban Countryside

Sheffield is blessed with an enormous variety of green spaces plus its own "lake district" to the west and north-west of the city where the valleys are occupied by reservoirs. The city's "heritage" public parks such as the Botanical Gardens, Norfolk Park, Firth Park, Weston Park, Endcliffe Park, Meersbrook Park, Hillsborough Park and Whiteley Woods were enriched in the 20th century with the acquisition of Millhouses Park, Graves Park and Whirlow Brook Park. The 80 ancient woodlands dotted about the city add a further dimension to the city's green attractions.

The Botanical Gardens
Opened in 1836 (but only to shareholders and subscribers except on special occasions until 1898) the Botanical Gardens were designed by Robert Marnock who, in 1840, became curator of the Royal Botanical Gardens in Regent's Park, London. Covering 19 acres, the gardens were restored with the help of a Lottery Fund award of £5m in 1997. The photographs on these pages show the gatehouse at the entrance to the gardens (below) and the restored glass pavilions (left). The garden has a restored bear pit which was home to two live bears until the 1870s.

Weston Park was created from the grounds of Weston Hall, an early 19th century house built by Thomas Harrison, an eminent Sheffield sawmaker. His two daughters inherited the Weston Hall estate and on their death it was bought by Sheffield Corporation for £18,000. The grounds were re-designed as a public park by Robert Marnock. The hall became Sheffield's first museum. It was rebuilt in 1935 and has recently undergone extensive refurbishment funded by the Heritage Lottery Fund. The park and museum were officially opened in September 1875. The *Sheffield Daily Telegraph* reported that the park "was thronged by a well-behaved and highly delighted crowd. The weather was fine. The park looked in its gayest summer dress". By the 1980s and 1990s this strategically located park (it lies next to the University of Sheffield and the Children's Hospital) had become very neglected but a Lottery Fund award has allowed it to benefit from a much needed facelift.

▼ Meersbrook Park The land on which Meersbrook Park stands was purchased by Sheffield Corporation in 1886 to prevent it from being acquired for housing and to provide something more than just a place in which to promenade. Originally it included an ornamental rose garden, and a rockery with a cascade walk in an area known as The Glen, crossed by a rustic bridge. But these attractions have now mostly been lost. However the park is still handsome, with wonderful views across the city (below) and a walled garden that provides training and volunteering opportunities.

▶ Bishops' House Museum
Tucked away at the top of Meersbrook Park, this is the best surviving timber-framed house in Sheffield. Built about 1500 for a yeoman farmer-scythemaker, its interior contains many of its original features and looks just as it would have done in the 17th century, giving a flavour of life in Stuart England. The wonderful timber work can be examined at close quarters, inside and out. From the leafy Meersbrook Park there are stunning views across the entire city to the north. The park boasts a second historic building – Meersbrook House, built in 1780 by Benjamin Roebuck.

Hillsborough Park This park was originally the grounds of Hillsborough House, built in 1779 for Thomas Steade. In the 19th century it was successively in the ownership of John Rodgers of Joseph Rodgers & Sons, cutlery manufacturers, and the Dixon family, of the silverware and silver-plating company. Sheffield Corporation bought Hillsborough Park (excluding the hall) in 1890 and opened it as a public park in 1892. In 1903 the hall was also purchased and opened as a branch library. The lake in the park, an enlarged version of the original lake, was used for boating until about 1960. It is now a haven for wildlife and is used for fishing. A special feature of the park is the former walled kitchen garden. Work to restore this garden was begun by volunteers in 1991. It was re-opened by the Duke of Kent on 15 April 1993, the anniversary of the Hillsborough Stadium disaster in which 96 football supporters died. A Memorial Garden in the walled garden commemorates their lives.

▲ **Whirlow Brook Park** Lying four miles to the south-west of the city centre is the Limb valley with Whirlow Brook Park at its southern end. Whirlow Brook Park was purchased by the Town Trustees and the JG Graves Charitable Trust in 1946 and presented to the city. It was opened to the public in June 1951. Whirlow Brook House was built in 1906 by Mr and Mrs Percy Fawcett. Mr Fawcett's sister and husband, Mr and Mrs Walter Benton Jones, moved into the house in 1920 and invited the Royal Horticultural Society to advise on planting and planning the grounds during the late 1920s. The gardens that were created, so typical of the time, remain just about intact. There is a rock garden constructed of millstone grit, two pools and a lower lake. The house is now a restaurant. Continuing up the valley the path leads through mixed woodlands and eventually into much more open ground with young birch and hawthorn and wet pastureland and heath. The stream is boulder-strewn and most attractive.